TRAE YOUN

THE INSPIRATIONAL STORY OF HOW TRAE YOUNG BECAME ONE OF THE NBA'S TOP TALENTS

By

JACKSON CARTER

Copyright © 2022

Table of Contents

Table of Contents

Legal Notes

What Make A Great Point Guard?

A Team In Need of A Hero

Growing Up In Lubbock, Texas

A Basketball Family

Want To Be Just Like Dad

Creating His Own Legacy

Boomer Sooner

An Explosive Start to the NBA

Living The Dream

The Quest To Represent The USA

Life Off The Court

Giving Back To the Community

Three Stripe Life: Trae Young's Partnership With Adidas

Where Does Trae Young Stand In Comparison To Other Stars

How Trae Young Feels About Being Compared to Other Players

More From Jackson Carter Biographies

Other Works By Jackson Carter Biographies

Legal Notes

Trae Young is meant for entertainment and educational use only. All attempts have been made to present factual information in an unbiased context.

© 2022 Broad Base Publishing

All rights reserved. No portion of this book may be reproduced in any form without permission from the publisher, except as permitted by U.S. copyright law. For permissions contact:

BroadBasePublishing@Gmail.com

Introduction

Trying to sum up the life of a basketball player who is just starting his career is almost impossible. Trae Young, the current point guard for the Atlanta Hawks, is still in his early 20s as of 2022.

Despite his brand-new career within professional basketball, Young has proven time and again that he is a force to be reckoned with. In fact, basketball aficionados everywhere are already familiar with Young's rookie accomplishments. However, those with less knowledge about the NBA may not know who Trae Young is and how he's taking the NBA world by storm.

Young hasn't gotten to the same level as other pro basketball players like Steph Curry or Michael Jordan as a newbie to the professional basketball world. But, if Young continues with his success at the rate he's going, he'll get there in no time.

In fact, as of 2021, Trae Young leads the NBA in total points scored with a total of 657 points and counting. This means that he's even beat out the likes of Zach LaVine and Steph Curry.

Young hasn't let his quick success get to his head, though. In fact, he's an honorary board member of The Children's Center Rehabilitation Hospital in Oklahoma City, and he's also partnered with organizations to help eliminate the medical debt owed by low-income families. Young keeps his head on his shoulders and constantly thinks about others in a world where stardom and fame can easily get into your head.

It should come as no surprise that Young is an incredible basketball player. After all, it's in his blood. Trae Young's father was a professional basketball player in Europe. Additionally, Young also has an uncle who played college basketball through the NAIA.

Young's love for basketball has followed him throughout his life and is a constant fuel for his passion, which keeps him going. As he continues to break records and earn professional accolades, Young will continue down the path to becoming a household name. But before we dive deeper into Young's life, it's important to know and understand what a point guard does exactly and why this position is important in basketball.

Having a solid understanding of the point guard position will show you just how important the role is in basketball and how Young plays a major role in his team's success.

What Make A Great Point Guard?

A team's point guard runs the offense and is in charge of guarding the opposing team's point guard in an attempt to steal the ball. The point guard is a position given to the player who is generally considered the best dribbler and passer on the team.

In essence, the point guard is the strategic captain of the team. They need to know who is open to receiving the ball in order to make a shot. The point guard has to be hyperaware at all times to ensure he passes the ball to the right player at the right time.

Point guards work closely with their team's coach and are commonly referred to as the "quarterback" of the basketball world. They're also the most common position to receive an MVP award in the league.

Among the most famous point guards in NBA history to receive an MVP award are the iconic Magic Johnson, Allen Iverson, and Stephen Curry, to name a few. In fact, Magic Johnson won the NBA's MVP award three times throughout his career, and Stephen Curry has won this accolade twice so far.

After a team makes a basket, the point guard is the position responsible for bringing the ball down court to begin the next play. In general, point guards are judged more by their assist totals rather than the number of baskets they score. However, you'll find that many point guards still have a good track record in terms of points scored.

A good point guard will have good speed and preciseness, as well as excellent situational awareness skills and the ability to work together with their team. Some people argue that the point guard position is the most difficult of the five primary positions in basketball.

Not only do point guards have to be hyperaware while on the court, but they also need to project excellent leadership skills in order to keep their teammates engaged during gameplay.

As both the passer and scorer in the team, the added responsibilities of the point guard can make it a stressful position to fulfill. Point guards have the heavy responsibility of constantly weighing whether or not a decision is the right one. Without a proper risk assessment, the point guard may unintentionally freeze out his teammates and create a toxic team environment.

With that said, the point guard position in basketball is great for players who feel a need to maintain control of any situation. During gameplay, the ball is in the point guard's possession for the majority of the game. This gives point guards ample opportunity to assess every play and decide which is best at that moment.

The most well-known and decorated point guard in NBA history is none other than the iconic Magic

Johnson. Johnson can boast of carrying five different NBA titles, three Finals MVP awards, three NBA MVP awards, nine All-NBA first-team selections, and 12 different All-Star titles.

OFFENSE ROLE

Point guards are typically positioned around the perimeter when on the offensive side of a game. This spot gives them the best visual field in order to see all possible plays at that moment. As their primary goal is to scope out who is open to making a shot, point guards must exude great leadership skills on the court.

While in possession of the ball, the point guard needs to be nimble and quick to open themselves up to either shoot the ball or pass to the closest open player. Additionally, a good point guard must be able to make successful passes for their team to maintain possession of the ball.

You'll often find that good point guards also have an effective jump shot. For example, we all know Steph Curry for his ability to make jump shots as far away as half-court and sometimes further. Many point guards are beginning to adopt a more modern style of the position where scoring has become just as important as assisting another position.

DEFENSIVE ROLE

Point guards are typically positioned around the perimeter on the defensive front just as they were on the offensive. During defensive play, the point guard is responsible for defending against the opposing team's point guard in an attempt to steal the ball back for their team.

During this time, the point guard's job is to put consistent pressure on the opposing point guard and cause them to become ineffective at passing to another player. You may also find that defensive point guards also put pressure on other players on the court to keep them from successfully catching a pass.

A few current NBA players have become known for their defensive tactics as a point guard. These players include Jrue Holiday, Mike Conley Jr., Marcus Smart, and Chris Paul.

Despite the records held by some of the most well-known point guards in NBA history, there's no doubt that Trae Young will reach and exceed the current records.

A Team In Need of A Hero

The Atlanta Hawks are a professional American basketball team in the NBA. In fact, the Hawks are among the original teams established when the NBA was first formed back in 1949. The team was originally founded in Moline and Rock Island, Illinois, and Davenport, Iowa. Back then, they were known as the tri-city Blackhawks in 1946.

Before the founding of the NBA, the team played three seasons in the National Basketball League. Eventually, they relocated to Milwaukee, Wisconsin, before the 1951-1952 season, and that's when they changed the name from Blackhawks to simply "Hawks."

Though they didn't see big success for a long time, the team eventually drafted Bob Pettit, the future Hall of Famer, during the 1954 draft with a second overall pick. The Hawks moved from Wisconsin to Missouri in 1955 and made it to the NBA finals during the 1956-1957 basketball season.

The Hawks lost to the Boston Celtics during that final after playing seven games. During the next season's finals, the Hawks played the Celtics again and won. That win earned them their very first playoff title.

In 1968, the Hawks were sold to a group in Georgia where the team hosted some NBA stars. Pete Maravich, Walt Bellamy, and Lou Hudson were among those early Atlanta stars. It wasn't until 1982 that the Atlanta-based team would achieve bigger success.

In 1982, rookie Domonique Wilkins joined the Atlanta Hawks and led the team to four consecutive 50-win seasons during the 1980s.

After a while, the Hawks reached a dry spell where they didn't see a postseason playoff game until the late 2000s. While they began to earn playoff spots again, they still didn't see a playoff win during this revival.

Fast forward to 2014-2015, the team broke through and won a franchise-record of 60 games and advanced to the Eastern Conference finals. Although the Hawks ended up losing to the Cleveland Cavaliers, that season raised the morale of the team immensely.

Despite this, the team lost several good players and ended up in a last-place divisional finish during the 2017-2018 season. However, it would be just one year later when they would draft a point guard that could mark a major turning point for the Atlanta Hawk's team luck. That point guard is none other than Trae Young himself.

Growing Up In Lubbock, Texas

Rayford Trae Young was born in Lubbock, Texas, on September 19, 1998. Although his first name is Rayford, Young tends to go by his middle name, which is what the basketball world knows him as. Trae Young is black and white biracial, and has grown up with the love for basketball coursing through his veins.

Young's father, Rayford Young II, played professional basketball in Europe and Trae Young also has an uncle who played college basketball for the NAIA. Young's grandfather, Rayford Young I, is who inspired Young III to pursue a career in basketball as his grandpa was a star basketball player while in high school during the 1970s.

Young III was born while Young II was a junior guard for the basketball team at Texas Tech. Before retiring and moving into the medical sales industry, Trae Young's father played professionally in France, Italy, Portugal, and Spain.

Young's mother, Candice, was born to a family of pastors in Lubbock and met Young II while in high school. The high school sweethearts followed each other to Texas Tech, and shortly after, Trae was born.

Along with Trae, the Youngs have three other children. Trae's siblings are named Camryn, Timothy, and Caitlyn. Although Young was born in Lubbock, Texas, he and his family spent most of his childhood in Norman, Oklahoma. Out of his three siblings, Trae is exceptionally close to his younger brother, Timothy.

The family moved to Norman, Oklahoma so that Young II could pursue his graduate assistant position at Oklahoma for the coach at the time, Kelvin Sampson.

While growing up, Young was a big fan of the Canadian Professional Basketball Player, Steve Nash. Nash played in the NBA for 18 seasons and earned the NBA All-Star title eight times. Nash was also a seven-time All-NBA selection. With a role model like Steve Nash to look up to, it's unsurprising that Trae Young chose the path he did.

A Basketball Family

In addition to having a talented and driven professional NBA player to look up to while growing up, Trae Young also had support and encouragement from a long line of family members who love and appreciate the game.

Young has spoken many times about how his grandfather, Rayford Young I, inspired him to pursue a career in basketball. Because Trae's parents had him while they were still young and his father was still playing professional basketball, Trae spent a lot of time around his grandfather.

While Trae's father encouraged him to make it all the way to the NBA, Rayford I is the primary source of support. Young III has publicly spoken about how his grandfather is the one who fully encouraged him to be the first one in the family to "make it all the way."

Young's grandfather was also the first person to teach him how to shoot a basket. When Trae was just a toddler, Rayford I attached a Nerf basketball hoop to the back of one of the doors inside their house. He began teaching Trae how to properly shoot a basket from that day forward.

In fact, his grandfather has told several stories about how Trae would eventually graduate to various trick shots around the room. Among these stories are accounts of moments when Trae would shoot the ball from across the room on the couch.

Trae would rebound the ball and pass it to his grandfather to make the shot in other instances. Thus, a point guard was born. So, while Trae became enamored with the game by watching his dad play ball, his grandfather is the one who introduced the game to him in the first place.

As a basketball-loving family, the Youngs had a special family tradition during the holidays to watch NBA games all day and argue over which player was the best of all time. Trae would regularly argue in LeBron James' favor, while his grandfather was adamant about Julius Irving holding that title. Trae's father's choice was always in favor of Michael Jordan.

Basketball isn't Young's only love, though. While spending his childhood with his grandfather, the duo regularly listened to R&B slow jams together. While hanging out, the pair would often turn on New Edition, Boyz II Men, and Bobby Brown.

Young I also preached the importance of focusing on doing well in school and avoiding anything that could get him sidetracked. Trae's grandfather is also the one who initially gave Trae the talk that is common in Black families. This talk was the notion that Trae needed to work twice as hard as his white counterparts to get where he wanted to be in life.

Because the area Young III grew up in was predominantly white, he knew he needed to work much harder than his classmates to receive even half of the recognition they would.

Young I died when Trae was just ten years old, and Trae regularly talks about how his grandfather made a great impact on his life. In fact, Young III visits his grandfather's gravesite on the anniversary of his death every year to pay respects and keep him updated.

WANT TO BE JUST LIKE DAD

While Young III's grandfather was the cornerstone of Trae's love and adoration for basketball, watching his father play professionally also impacted his choices. Rayford Young II played basketball in both college and professionally. Like his son, Young II was also a point guard and played throughout all four years of his college career at Texas Tech. Trae's father's college basketball career lasted from 1996 to 2000. He was a starter for three out of four of his seasons and played in a total of 108 college basketball games.

In that time, he scored a total of 1,528 points and was able to rack up 407 assists during his college career. Additionally, Young II was also an excellent 3-point shooter with a 37.9% clip on his record.

Young III had the opportunity to watch his dad during his dad's best game with the Texas Tech team. During the game, Young II scored 41 points against the Kansas Jayhawks, and the duo still talks about that game to this day.

Trae and his dad remain incredibly close to this day. During one father's-day game, Young III threw his winning jersey up to his father in the stands to which his father responded by blowing him a kiss and shaking his fist with pride.

In addition to his college career with Texas Tech, Rayford Young II went on to play professionally in Europe. Young II played professionally in France,

Italy, Portugal, and Spain during his European career. Young II eventually switched career paths and earned his Ph.D. before starting his own medical equipment business.

Along with his father, Trae Young also has an uncle who played college basketball at the Junior College and NAIA levels.

Creating His Own Legacy

Trae Young attended Norman North Highschool in Norman, Oklahoma, where he graduated in 2016.

Although Young III has always had an unwavering adoration for the game of basketball, he didn't join his high school team right away. Rather than joining the team during his freshman year, Young III waited until he was a sophomore in high school to start playing high school basketball.

Trae Young certainly lived up to everyone's expectations during his first season as a sophomore. He ended the sophomore season with an average of 25 points, four rebounds, and five assists per game. This performance helped him to earn the Oklahoma's sophomore of the year title.

During his junior year in basketball, Young III drastically improved. His efficiency during gameplay improved immensely and he rounded out the year with an average of 34.2 points, 4.6 assists, and 4.6 rebounds. This improvement helped the team to win the Oklahoma's class 6a championship trophy.

His senior year was even better. Young III achieved an average of 42.6 points during his senior season compared to his previous year. Young III also racked up an average of 5.8 rebounds and earned the McDonald's All-American Honor. In addition to that, Young III was also named to the Jordan Brand Classic.

By the end of high school, Trae Young had racked up a total of 2,445 points, 268 rebounds, 365 assists, and 225 steals during his three-year high school basketball career. Young III led his team to a 24-4 record and led the high school team to win the regional title as well as the 2016 Oklahoma championship.

While still in high school, Young III earned several awards and accolades pertaining to basketball. Among those awards and accolades are the 2016 USA Today All-USA Oklahoma Player of the Year, the 2016 Gatorade Oklahoma Boys Basketball Player of the Year, 2016 MaxPreps Junior All-American Second Team, 2016 Oklahoma Player of the Year, 2015 Oklahoma Sophomore of the Year, 2015 All-Region, and the 2015 Conference Offensive Player of the Year.

Young III's high school career would naturally bring several college ball scouts to his games and would eventually lead him to choose the University of Oklahoma. The nickname "ice Trae" would surface during his high school career. This nickname stemmed from the idea that Trae Young was always ice cold while on the court.

With such a rich and extensive family background revolving around basketball, Young III's success in bringing his team to the championships should come as no surprise. Even during high school, Trae Young has always been considered a force to be reckoned with. His impeccable scoring, assisting, and rebounding records attracted several different universities and colleges to seek his recruitment.

Young III's unwavering love and talent for the game of basketball earned him potential spots at several colleges and universities. However, the University of Kentucky, Oklahoma State, and the University of Kansas were among his top picks, next to the University of Oklahoma. It seems that Young III has a sweet spot for home as he chose to remain at home during his college basketball career.

Young III's jersey is currently retired and hanging in the halls of Norman North High School to commemorate the former student's success.

By the end of his high school career, Young III earned the title of Five-Star Point Guard and was ranked as the number 15 recruit in the entire country.

In 2016, Trae Young had the opportunity to travel to Chile to compete in the FIBA America U18 Championship. His team went on to win the gold medal at this championship. This opportunity, in addition to his stellar high school record, gave him the five-star point guard title. These accolades made him a star recruit for the University of Oklahoma.

Boomer Sooner

Once Young III committed to the University of Oklahoma to play for the Sooners, he recorded his first double-double in 2017. A double-double refers to a single-game accomplishment where a player scores ten or more in at least two out of the five statistical categories. These categories are points, rebounds, assists, steals, and blocked shots.

During that same year, Young III tied the NCAA single-game assists record of 22, where he and his team beat the Northwestern State Demons by 26 points.

Trae Young only played for the University of Oklahoma Sooners for one season before he was recruited into the NBA. However, his one year of college basketball allowed him to polish his skill set and bring his expertise into the professional world of the NBA.

During his freshman year at the University of Oklahoma, Young III played and started in 32 games. His averages were 35.4 minutes of gameplay, 27.4 points scored per game, 3.9 rebounds per game, 8.7 assists per game, and 1.7 steals per game. Trae Young shot 42.2% from the field, 36% from the three-point range, and 86.1% from the foul line.

Young III also earned the title of the first NCAA player to lead the nation in scoring and assists in Division I history. He was also named consensus All-American first team, Wayman Tisdale National Freshman of the Year, a unanimous vote for the All-Big 12 First Team, and the Big 12 Conference Freshman and Newcomer of the Year.

Trae Young's scoring average was the highest in Big 12 history, and his per-game assist record is ranked second on the all-time list.

Young III had four games with a recorded score total of 40 points or more, but he also became the first major conference player in the history of the NCAA to rack up 800 points and 250 assists in a single season.

Trae Young's performance during his single-year college basketball career led many experts to compare him to the likes of Blake Griffin and Buddy Hield, two other professional NBA players who also attended the University of Oklahoma.

After his freshman year basketball season, Young III was already being considered by several teams in the NBA draft. His talents are often compared to another incredibly talented point guard in the NBA, Steph Curry from the Golden State Warriors.

Trae Young's talent was so prominent after his first season in college that he was drafted by the Dallas Mavericks as the 5th overall pick. However, that's not where Young III ended up. In 2018, Trae Young was traded to the Atlanta Hawks for Luka Doncic, a Slovenian basketball player.

Although Trae Young's grandfather has been gone for several years, we're sure he's incredibly proud of his grandson for reaching the goal so carefully set out for him.

An Explosive Start to the NBA

Trae Young eventually accepted a rookie contract deal with the Atlanta Hawks. This deal stipulated that Young III would earn a salary of $15,167,700 during the first three years of his contract. According to some reports, Young III was traded to the Atlanta Hawks as the Hawks and the Mavericks have a deal, which states that Young III will never play for the Mavericks.

This elusive deal led to the initial trade and guaranteed a protected future first-round pick. Young III began playing for the Atlanta Hawks in 2018 and is still a part of the professional team.

During his first season in the NBA, Young III played and started in 81 NBA basketball games. He averaged 30.9 minutes of gameplay per game, 19.1 points per game, 3.7 rebounds per game, and 8.1 assists per game.

His rookie year saw him shooting at 41.8% from the field, 32.4% from the 3-point line, and 82.9% from the foul line. Among all of the qualifying NBA rookies, Young III ranked first in assists and fourth overall in the NBA. He also ranked second in points per game and 34th in the NBA, second in free throw percentages, third in minutes per game, sixth in steals per game, and 10th in rebounds per game.

His 2019-2020 season saw slightly less overall gameplay as he played and started in 60 games. Despite playing fewer games, Young III had a career-high in terms of minutes played per game with 35.3 minutes, which put him at 10th in the NBA.

During the 2019-2020 season, he scored a career-high 29.6 points per game, ranking him fourth in the NBA. He also had a career-high in rebounds with 4.3 per game, 9.3 assists per game, and 1.1 steals per game.

He also shot career-highs in each facet of scoring with 43.7% from the field, 36.1% from the 3-point line, and 86% from the foul line.

During the 2020-2021 NBA basketball season, Trae Young played and started in 63 games, and averaged 33.7 minutes of gameplay per game. His other averages included 25.3 points per game, 3.9 rebounds per game, a career-high 9.4 assists per game, and 0.8 steals per game.

He also shot career-highs in each facet of scoring, beating out his previous year's career-high. His averages were 43.8% from the field, 34.3% from the 3-point line, and 88.6% from the foul line. These records helped Trae Young to rank 19th in the entire NBA for efficiency during gameplay.

Overall, Trae Young has played and started in a total of 204 games with a total of 6,748 minutes of gameplay. To this day, he's scored 4,921 points, had 667 rebounds, completed 1,807 assists, and 190 steals while playing. He accomplished all of this, in addition to a shooting range of 43.1% from the field,

34.3% from the 3-point line, and 86.1% from the foul line.

Young III has already earned serious accolades in his three seasons in the NBA. These accolades include being named a starter for the Eastern Conference in the 2020 NBA All-Star Game and recording the only double-double in the entire contest. Young III had ten points and a game-high 10 assists during the game, all within 16 minutes.

He was unanimously chosen for the All-Rookie first team during his rookie year, was named Eastern Conference Player of the Week three separate times, and was a four-time rookie of the month selection in the NBA.

LIVING THE DREAM

Trae Young's passion for the game of basketball brought him to the goal he and his grandfather discussed a long time ago, but it has also helped him to achieve some serious milestones within just three seasons of playing in the NBA.

During his first postseason appearance of the year, Trae Young became the second player, behind LeBron James, in the history of the NBA to gather at least 30 points, ten assists, and five boards during a postseason debut.

He also recorded 32 points and ten assists at one point, which led him to become the fourth player in NBA history to tally up at least 30 points and ten assists during their debut. Young III also scored 30 points during his second playoff game. This accomplishment led him to become the first player in Atlanta Hawks history to score that many points in both his first two postseason appearances.

During the 2019-2020 season, Young III led the entire Eastern Conference in assists, recording a total of 560 assists in two consecutive seasons.

Consistently raising his point averages per game has also earned Trae Young more recognition. In fact, Young III's increase is the second-most in NBA history, averaging at least 19 points per game in at least 60 games played.

Also, during the 2019-2020 season, Young III had an average of 29.6 points per game, which is the most for an NBA sophomore since the early-mid 1970s.

Trae Young also became the fifth player in NBA history to average at least 29 points per game as well as at least nine assists per game. He is the first player in NBA history to compile at least 38 points, nine assists, and seven rebounds in his team's first two games of the season.

When Young III scored a career-high 50 points during the game against Miami in 2020, he became the first player in NBA history to score at least 50 points in 12 shots or less and less than 20 free throws.

Trae Young also made 156 3-point shots, which is the most in Atlanta rookie history. Those shots are also the second-most in NBA history made by a rookie who is 20 years old or younger. Lastly, Young III became the third rookie to ever score at least 19.1 points per game and has at least eight assists per game.

The Quest To Represent The USA

At this point, Trae Young has become a household name to basketball enthusiasts everywhere. This stardom has come from the fact that many feel he carried his team to the 2021 Eastern Conference finals. It's impossible to deny that Young III has the talent needed to represent the United States at an international level.

In 2021, Trae Young was named a finalist for the USA National Team and the 2021 U.S. Olympic Men's Team. However, he was snubbed on the court and didn't make the cut. This caused quite a controversy amongst the basketball community, including Trae Young himself.

Young III knows he's talented and expressed disappointment and frustration about being snubbed from the USA Men's Basketball Team despite having plenty of talent to succeed. In fact, Young III even took to social media to explain his feelings about feeling like he's constantly being overlooked for these types of opportunities.

The USA team roster had sparked a lot of debate, especially among those who had seen the players on the roster. For instance, players like Khris Middleton and Zach LaVine were considered over Trae Young. Young III expressed frustration because he met all the necessary criteria and was still overlooked during the entire process.

Despite the snub from the 2021 USA Men's Basketball Team, Young III has earned several accolades that make him an excellent representative of NBA basketball. In addition to his 2016 participation on the USA Men's U18 Championship team, he also had a qualifying top-four finish that propelled him into the 2017 FIBA U19 World Championship. Young III played in all five games in the championship and averaged six points per game, 3.6 rebounds per game, and 3.2 assists per game.

In October of 2016, he also participated in the 2016 USA Basketball Men's Junior National Team minicamp.

In 2019, Trae Young was a select team member who trained both with and against the 2019 National Team during the preparation for the 2019 FIBA World Cup.

It seems many naysayers claim that Young III only got to where he is by luck. However, the countless accomplishments we've seen him achieve prove those negative people wrong.

Despite starting in the 2020 NBA All-Star Game, Trae Young wasn't invited back the following year. This may not seem like a big deal. However, players were consistently dropping out, and Young III never received a call to play as a replacement. Again, this may not seem like much of a snub but the game was slated to be played in Atlanta, Young III's "home" city.

In addition to that, Young III also only earned two votes for the third-team All-NBA game. To top everything off, the list of available players kept decreasing due to prior engagements, and Trae Young was still left in the proverbial dust.

Although Trae Young was overlooked for the USA team, he wasn't embarrassed despite having all the right qualifications and star power. On the other hand, this made those who chose the players for the USA Men's team look incompetent.

Trae Young's size is much smaller than many other basketball players currently in the NBA. Because of that, Young III has to be creative in his gameplay and strategy. By taking a few notes from Kobe Bryant, Young III learned how to use his opponents' size against them.

However, the rules in the NBA are constantly being changed and rearranged. During the 2020-2021 NBA season, NBA officials reviewed and tweaked the rule book. This was their response to Young III's creativity on the court. Rather than encourage defensive teams to get better, they made the rules more relaxed, giving bigger players the advantage again.

These relaxed rules make Trae Young look like one of the worst defenders in the NBA according to many sports media personnel. However, what his size lacks in defensive skills, he makes up for on the offensive.

Additionally, Young III used his size to his advantage. While many other point guards are bigger players, Young III takes a page out of Steve Nash's book by setting his opponents up to take fouls. In fact, during one game against the team Steve Nash coaches, Young III set his defender up to take a foul.

He did this by getting his defender behind him before stopping abruptly. By doing this, his defender ran right into him and was called out on a foul. Some players and coaches, including Nash himself, are against this type of gameplay. However, smaller players like Trae Young utilize this strategy to get a leg up on their competition.

LIFE OFF THE COURT

Despite his unwavering love for basketball, Young is also a devout Christian and is currently engaged to his longtime girlfriend and partner, Shelby Miller. Young III and Miller met while Trae Young played basketball at the University of Oklahoma in 2017. Miller was a cheerleader for the University of Oklahoma Sooners, and that was how she crossed paths with Young III.

Trae Young was also featured on the second season of Young Hollywood's original docuseries titled Rookie on the Rise. This docuseries followed Young III on his path to winning the Rookie of the Year.

In addition to actively making appearances on his fiancé's TikTok account, Trae Young is also active on Instagram. The couple announced their engagement in December of 2021 on Instagram, and many of Trae Young's teammates and opponents congratulated the couple on their engagement.

While we know Shelby Miller as Trae Young's fiancé, there's more to her story than simply "Trae's fiancé." Miller was raised in Norman, Oklahoma, just like Young III. Her mother works at the University of Oklahoma and her father works in automotive maintenance. Shelby Miller has one sister named Cassie and a niece.

Miller was born on October 25, 1995, and graduated from the University of Oklahoma with a degree in

Communications and Media in 2019. Though she's an accomplished dancer, she's most notably known for being a cheerleader during Young III's short college career.

Like Young III, Miller is also a practicing Christian. Miller lives in Atlanta with Young III and the couple is active on Tiktok. Miller owns two French bulldogs named Normi and Lanta, likely named after her two home cities.

GIVING BACK TO THE COMMUNITY

The Trae Young Family Foundation was founded in 2019 with the aim of continuing the education on mental health problems among children and adults. The organization places a big focus on eradicating cyber and social media bullying.

Because cyberbullying can lead to a plethora of mental health issues, from PTSD to depression and anxiety, the foundation strives to inspire and help positively impact children and adults from all walks of life.

The Trae Young Family Foundation idea originally sprouted in Young III's mind during his youth in Oklahoma. When Young III noticed that professional basketball players were doing great things in their communities, he was inspired to do the same thing once he made it into the NBA too.

The foundation is currently working on a big undertaking with the Norman Multisport and Aquatic project. This project came to fruition when Young III realized he had to have his parents drive him to faraway places to partake in opportunities to hone his gifts and abilities in basketball and other sports.

Young III didn't want other families to have to take on that kind of burden. Instead, he and the foundation came up with the idea to build an athletic complex that allows families in Norman to get high-quality instruction and practice to help build their skills in a variety of sports.

The project was established in July of 2020 and the Trae Young Family Foundation has pledged four million dollars to see the project to completion. In February of 2021, the city council in Norman approved the advancement of the project, which tacked on an additional $920,250 toward the project's budget.

Because Trae and his sisters grew up incredibly active in sports, and with their youngest sibling, Timothy, still active, this project is more important to the family than ever. The creation of this multisport and aquatic complex will allow Norman to become a hub for multiple sporting events.

In turn, families do not have to travel far outside of the city often to give their kids the same opportunities the Young siblings had growing up.

Although the primary goal of the athletic center is to give kid and teen athletes a place to attend and participate in state and national sporting events, the center will also be open for recreational use.

A special scholarship program will be put into effect to ensure income isn't a burden for families who want to utilize the athletic complex. Young athletes that qualify for a scholarship through the multisport and aquatic center will be able to use it toward everything they need to excel in their sport, from jerseys to equipment and other fees.

With the help of the Norman City Council, the center has also enlisted help from the Columbus Corporation to help operate the facility. The Columbus Organization is more well-known as OKC's Santa Fe Family Life Center. This center will assist with the project by helping provide their experience with underprivileged families.

This partnership will give disadvantaged youth an equal opportunity to participate in the same activities as other families and adaptive sports like wheelchair basketball and volleyball.

In addition to the completion of this athletic complex, the Trae Young Family Foundation also hopes to host a scholarship program. This scholarship program will encourage students to do well in school by participating in various programs within the athletic center.

It was also announced by the Norman City Council that the foundation's multisport and aquatic center would have an exclusive healthcare partnership with Norman Regional Health System. NRHS has a 15-year lease with the building and will provide health services like physical therapy, athletic training, and strength and conditioning training too.

Because of his work through his family foundation, Trae has received NBA honors via the Community

Assist Award, the Jason Collier Memorial Trophy from the Hawks, and he's been vocal in the Silence the Shame campaign about Teen Mental Wellness.

In addition to the work currently being done by the Trae Young Family Foundation, Young III also helped eliminate one million dollars' worth of medical debt for struggling Atlanta families in 2020. Trae Young donated this money through his foundation and helped more than 570 families free themselves from their medical debt burdens.

Aside from using his financial privilege for good, Trae Young has also been extremely vocal about a variety of causes he cares about. These causes include COVID vaccination campaigns, granting clemency for Julius Jones, and being a vocal supporter of the Black Lives Matter movement.

Along with the rest of his Hawks team, Trae Young partnered with the Silence the Shame movement to raise awareness about mental health problems among teens today. The Hawks team did this in the form of a Teen Mental Wellness Courtside Chat. This chat was hosted by the founder of Silence the Shame, Shanti Das.

Along with Das, Young III was also joined by recording artist, Chloe Bailey. During the event, Young III discussed and stressed the importance of the cause and helped to raise awareness about it being okay to talk to someone if you feel like you're struggling.

In addition to this courtside chat, the Atlanta Hawks also hosted a pre-game panel discussion titled "Sports, Entertainment, and Mental Wellness." This panel educated attendees about how mental illness affects everyone, including those in the limelight. It also explained how each of the three things is interconnected with each other.

To expand on this partnership, Young III and his team also plan to host student groups in May. May is a significant month in the world of mental wellness as it's Mental Health Awareness Month.

Three Stripe Life: Trae Young's Partnership With Adidas

Trae Young signed with Adidas when he began his NBA career back in 2018. Because his profile and stardom have continued to rise since then, his first official shoe design was released in September of 2021.

Young III wore his first original sneaker design during the 2021 NBA playoffs. Before that, he religiously wore Adidas's Harden models before becoming the face of Adidas's N3XT L3V3L sneaker line. This sneaker line is described as futuristic and has Lightstrike foam cushioning without laces.

His first sneaker, the Trae Young 1, debuted during his first game of the NBA playoffs at Madison Square Garden. The timing was incredible for the Adidas brand as Young III showed the best of his skills during this game.

Throughout the spring and summer of 2021, Young III showcased a variety of color schemes for his Adidas shoe design, with the most sought-after schemes "The 1996 Olympics," Icee, and Team USA. Additionally, his debut colorway was meant to be inspired by his pets.

The Trae Young 1 is vastly different from the N3XT L3V3L construction. For starters, the shoe is low cut and features laces. However, the laces are semi-concealed by a shroud. For cushioning inside of the

Trae Young 1's, Adidas uses a mix of Lightstrike and BOOST on top of a semi-translucent outsole.

The semi-translucent outsole features a multi-directional traction pattern, and there are pull tabs on the front and back of the ankle collar. These tabs feature Young's logo.

Trae Young 1's are priced at $140, making them the most expensive hoop shoe offered by the Adidas brand. There are five different colorways currently available to choose from. These colorways are ICEE, ICEE Cotton Candy, Peachtree, So So Def, and So So Def ATL.

WHERE DOES TRAE YOUNG STAND IN COMPARISON TO OTHER STARS

Trae Young is often compared to other successful NBA players like Steph Curry, Steve Nash, and James Harden, to name a few. This makes sense if you put each player's gameplay side by side with Young III's. When you do this, you'll see several similarities between them. With that said, the comparisons made between Trae Young and other successful NBA players were made for various reasons.

When Young III is compared to Steph Curry, it's usually in terms of both players' abilities to shoot successful baskets from the 3-point line and beyond. Although Young III is newer to the NBA basketball scene, he's been able to outperform Steph Curry on several occasions. Many basketball experts have expressed the belief that Trae Young is poised to become the next Steph Curry in terms of 3-point shots.

In fact, Young III has already surpassed Curry in average points per game. While Curry averages 24.3 points per game, Young III takes the lead with 25.3 points per game. Young III also surpasses Curry when it comes to assists per game with an average of 9.1, while Curry rounds out at 6.5.

While Steph Curry has had a longer NBA run and maintains the lead in best season stats, Young III passes Curry in best season averages when it comes to assists per game. Curry's record for assists per game stands at 8.5, while Young III's record reigns supreme at 9.7 assists per game.

When comparing the two players' playoff stats, Trae Young surpasses Steph Curry in total points scored per game with an average of 28.8 in comparison to Curry's 26.5. Young III also surpasses Curry in playoff stats in terms of assists per game. While Curry's assists per game average is 6.3, Young III's stands at 9.5.

TRAE YOUNG VS. STEVE NASH: STAT COMPARISONS

Trae Young has said on multiple occasions that Steve Nash greatly inspired him to pursue a professional basketball career. For that reason, it should come as no surprise that the two players are often compared to each other side by side.

Nash has almost two decades of experience as a professional basketball player in the NBA, so he rightfully has more awards and accolades than the newcomer, Trae Young. With that said, Young III has outperformed Nash in various aspects of the game.

Young III has surpassed Nash's records for NBA regular-season stats per game, for starters. While Steve Nash's points per game average sits at 14.3, Young III's reigns supreme at 25.3. Trae Young also has a slightly higher average number of rebounds per game with 3.9 to Nash's 3.0.

The same can also be said for both players' average assists per game. While Nash's average is 8.5, Young III passes Nash with a 9.1 average. In terms of steals, Young III wins with a 0.9 average over Nash's 0.7, and Young III's average number of blocks per game outperforms Nash with 0.2 compared to Nash's 0.1.

Although Nash has a higher number in total stats, Trae Young is on track to outperform Nash on an astronomical level.

So far, Young III has beat out Nash's best-season record in terms of points per game, rebounds per game, and steals per game. While Nash's best season saw 18.8 points per game, Young III's 29.6 ppg average is much higher. Young III's rebounds and steals per game best are slightly higher, with 4.3 to Nash's 4.2 rebounds and 1.1 to Nash's 1.0 in steals.

When looking at both players' stats in terms of NBA playoff games played, Young III outperforms Nash in points per game, assists per game, and steals per game. Young III's playoff stats are 28.8, 9.5, and 1.3, respectively, to Nash's 17.3, 8.8, and 0.6.

Young III reigns supreme in points per game and steals per game for best playoff game stats. Trae Young's best playoff game saw 28.8 points per game and 1.3 steals per game compared to Nash's 23.9 ppg record and 0.9 steals per game.

TRAE YOUNG VS. JAMES HARDEN: STAT COMPARISONS

Trae Young is also commonly compared to James Harden, likely because their stats and gameplay choices are so similar. Although Harden has almost ten years more of experience than Young III, the two players are continuously head to head when it comes to the regular season and playoff stats.

When it comes to NBA regular-season stats, Young III has a leg up on Harden in average points per game and average assists per game. While Harden boasts 24.9 points scored per game, Young III has a slight edge with an average of 25.3

For average assists per game, Young III beats out Harden with an average of 9.3 over Harden's 6.8. Both players' goal percentages are almost identical, with Harden having a minuscule edge in field goals and 3-point shots. However, Young III has a slightly higher percentage when it comes to free-throw shots.

Young III has yet to surpass Harden in terms of best game personal records, but Young III wins when it comes to per-game stats in the playoffs for points and assists per game. While Harden has an average of 23.3 points per game, Young III wins with 28.8. Trae Young's average assists per playoff game is a whopping 9.5, while Harden's sits at 6.0.

Harden has an edge on Young III for best playoff personal records in every aspect, except for assists per game. In this category, Young III has a record of 9.5 assists per game as opposed to Harden's 8.6.

TRAE YOUNG VS. DONOVAN MITCHELL: STAT COMPARISONS

Although Trae Young isn't compared to Donovan Mitchell, the two have roughly the same level of experience in the NBA. There are numerous comparisons between the two in the media and the internet.

When comparing NBA regular-season stats, Young III takes the lead in average points scored per game as well as average assists. In terms of points scored, Young III boasts 25.3 to Mitchell's 23.9. In terms of assists per game, Young III wins with 9.1 compared to Mitchell's average of 4.5.

Because Mitchell has one year of experience as Young III's senior, he does have a slight edge on total overall stats. However, Young III beats out Mitchell in total assists with 2,544 overall compared to Mitchell's 1,542.

Young III also has a better free throw percentage and beats Mitchell when it comes to best season records for points and assists per game. Young III's points per game best record reigns supreme at 29.6, while Mitchell's sits slightly lower at 26.4.

Additionally, Young III's assists per game best is 9.7, while Mitchell's is just 5.3 in that same year. The two players have tied in per game NBA playoff stats for points per game as well as steals per game. However, Young III's stats for assists per playoff game are much higher at 9.5 than Mitchell's 4.6 average.

When looking at total overall stats for both players, Young III has a slightly higher number of assists per game with 152 to Mitchell's 151. When looking at both players' best playoff games, Trae Young has a higher number of assists per game with a record of 9.5 in comparison to Mitchell's 5.5 records.

TRAE YOUNG VS. LUKA DONCIC: STAT COMPARISONS

When Trae Young was originally drafted, he was traded for Luka Doncic before ever playing for the team that originally drafted him. Young III also became the runner-up to Doncic when it came to voting for the best rookie player.

While Doncic has the upper hand on regular-season stats per game, Young III is better in terms of assists per game. Young III's assists per game average is 9.1 compared to Doncic's slightly lower 8.0 average.

Although Doncic has a higher point per game average, Young III is the winner when it comes to total points scored overall. While Doncic has an overall score of 6,962 points, Young III has a total of 7,076 to his name so far.

Young III also has a higher number of assists in his career with 2,544 to Doncic's 2,102. Trae Young has also played in more games than Luka Doncic with 280 games played to Doncic's 264.

Trae Young also has a higher percentage in 3-point and free-throw shots, and has a higher season-best 29.6 points per game compared to Doncic's 28.8 season-best. Young III also beats out Doncic on season-best in terms of assists per game with 9.7 to Doncic's 8.8.

When comparing the two players' NBA playoff stats, they are tied in assists per game with 9.5. Although Doncic has a slightly higher playoff average, Young III has a slight upper hand in steals per game with a 1.3 average compared to Doncic's 1.2 average.

Tallying up everything from both players' playoff runs shows that Young III has scored 461 total points compared to Doncic's 436. Young III also played in more games than Doncic, so this number accurately reflects that.

How Trae Young Feels About Being Compared to Other Players

Regarding the common comparisons Trae Young has heard in terms of who he is like the most on the court, the two names that regularly surface are Steph Curry and Steve Nash. Young III has publicly spoken about these comparisons and says that he feels his gameplay is closer to Steve Nash than Steph Curry.

These feelings from Trae Young likely come from the fact that he looked up to Steve Nash while he was growing up. In fact, he says that his choice of gameplay is heavily inspired by what he saw from Nash when he was younger.

This doesn't mean that Young III is completely writing off the Steph Curry comparisons. In fact, he says he does see some similarities in his gameplay to that of Curry's. However, he identifies more closely with Nash than with Curry.

MORE FROM JACKSON CARTER BIOGRAPHIES

My goal is to spark the love of reading in young adults around the world. Too often children grow up thinking they hate reading because they are forced to read material they don't care about. To counter this we offer accessible, easy to read biographies about sportspeople that will give young adults the chance to fall in love with reading.

Go to the Website Below to Join Our Community

https://mailchi.mp/7cced1339ff6/jcbcommunity

Or Find Us on Facebook at

www.facebook.com/JacksonCarterBiographies

As a Member of Our Community You Will Receive:

First Notice of Newly Published Titles

Exclusive Discounts and Offers

Influence on the Next Book Topics

Don't miss out, join today and help spread the love of reading around the world!

OTHER WORKS BY JACKSON CARTER BIOGRAPHIES

Patrick Mahomes: The Amazing Story of How Patrick Mahomes Became the MVP of the NFL

Donovan Mitchell: How Donovan Mitchell Became a Star for the Salt Lake City Jazz

Luka Doncic: The Complete Story of How Luka Doncic Became the NBA's Newest Star

The Eagle: Khabib Nurmagomedov: How Khabib Became the Top MMA Fighter and Dominated the UFC

Lamar Jackson: The Inspirational Story of How One Quarterback Redefined the Position and Became the Most Explosive Player in the NFL

Jimmy Garoppolo: The Amazing Story of How One Quarterback Climbed the Ranks to Be One of the Top Quarterbacks in the NFL

Zion Williamson: The Inspirational Story of How Zion Williamson Became the NBA's First Draft Pick

Kyler Murray: The Inspirational Story of How Kyler Murray Became the NFL's First Draft Pick

Do Your Job: The Leadership Principles that Bill Belichick and the New England Patriots Have Used to Become the Best Dynasty in the NFL

Turn Your Gaming Into a Career Through Twitch and Other Streaming Sites: How to Start, Develop and Sustain an Online Streaming Business that Makes Money

From Beginner to Pro: How to Become a Notary Public

Printed in Great Britain
by Amazon